#THIS IS NOT JOURNALISM

Ross Mueller

CURRENT THEATRE SERIES

First published in 2025
by Currency Press Pty Ltd,
Gadigal Land, Suite 310, 46–56 Kippax Street, Surry Hills, NSW 2010, Australia
enquiries@currency.com.au
www.currency.com.au

in association with Australian Writers Theatre

Typeset by Brighton Gray for Currency Press.
Printed by Fineline Print + Copy Services, Revesby, NSW.
Front cover shows Philip McGrath and Mark Pegler. Back cover shows Jack Andrew.
Cover design by Mathias Johansson for Currency Press

Currency Press acknowledges the Traditional Owners of the Country on which we live and work. We pay our respects to all Aboriginal and Torres Strait Islander Elders, past and present.

A catalogue record for this book is available from the National Library of Australia

Contents

I live and work on the land of the Awabakal people.
I pay my respects to Elders, past and present, and acknowledge all First Nations custodians of Country and their continuing connection to the land and waters across Australia.

R.M.

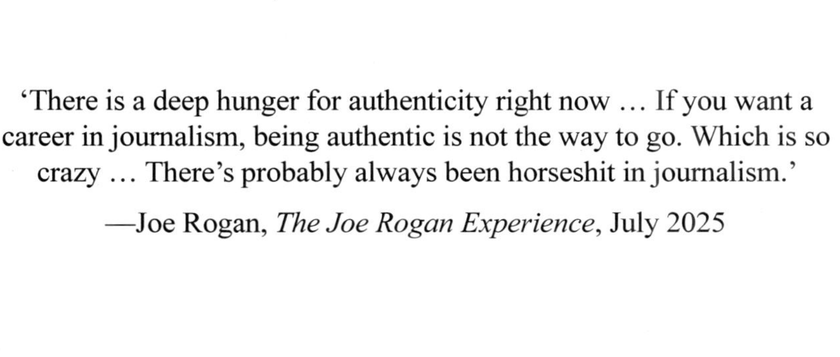

'There is a deep hunger for authenticity right now … If you want a career in journalism, being authentic is not the way to go. Which is so crazy … There's probably always been horseshit in journalism.'

—Joe Rogan, *The Joe Rogan Experience*, July 2025

#THIS IS NOT JOURNALISM was first presented by UpStage at the Playhouse and Australian Writers Theatre at Civic Theatre Playhouse, Awabakal and Worimi country, Newcastle, with the following cast and creatives:

OLIVER MADISON	Jack Andrew
ANDREW CARTER	Mark Peglar
PETER FRANCIS	Philip McGrath

Director, Ross Mueller
Lighting and Set Designer, Lyndon Buckley
Sound Designer, Ross Mueller
Dramaturg, Vanessa Bates

CHARACTERS

OLIVER MADISON, young producer.

ANDREW CARTER, Gen X cusp on-air talent.

PETER FRANCIS, booming consultant.

SETTING

It's Friday night in the Real Time News conference room. In the room next door, a party is starting for Brian Mathews to celebrate his fifty years in media.

RTN is a cable news station in decline. The conference room is untidy, with a small plastic folding table, a large whiteboard branded with vinyl lettering announcing 'RTN: CARTER: UNFILTERED SCHEDULE' and handwritten instruction, 'DO NOT REMOVE'.

For furniture, there is a single executive swivel chair, one Officeworks $12 folding chair, some boxes of wine for Brian's party, pair of boxing gloves and pads in one corner, a 12.5kg dumbbell in the other corner, a football, whiteboard cleaning detritus and screwed up balls of whiteboard inky paper. On the folding table there is a plate of sausage rolls and sauce, for Brian's party next door.

In the foreground, there is a neutral space. This is the airlock. It surrounds the conference room. Inside there are two live mics on straight stands. The mics are labelled with TV identification mic flags which simply say 'STORY'. The actors use these mics when they are sharing a secret or fabricating a story.

TEXT NOTE

The slash / is an interruption point, for overlaps.

This playtext went to press before the end of rehearsals and may differ from the play as performed.

ONE

Lights up in the airlock and the conference room. OLIVER *is in the airlock. Dressed for work, he wears a hat with the word UNFILTERED.* ANDREW *is in the conference room, sweating after playing squash.* OLIVER *has a digital recorder in his hand. He speaks into the live mic labelled STORY.*

OLIVER: [*to audience*] Andrew Carter lived on Friskies for three solid weeks. 'Starvation wages and Friskies for dinner.' Cat food was the only thing that kept this young newsman alive when he started here at Real Time News. Well, that's the origin story he told me. My name is Oliver Madison, and I am now Andrew Carter's producer. He goes on air at ten p.m., I start work at midday and every day, it is my job to find the next big story for him, pitch it, produce it, script it, get it on the teleprompter and get it out there. I love it, I love my job. The next big story is everything. And this, is how it begins.

TWO

ANDREW: This is serious!

OLIVER *bounds into the conference room.*

OLIVER: This is hectic! Breaking now!

ANDREW: Mate, I need your full / attention.

OLIVER: This is the story.

He illustrates on the whiteboard.

There is a geomagnetic storm happening in outer space right now.

ANDREW: What the fuck are you talking about?

OLIVER: It is like a massive solar storm, and it has the potential to knock out thousands of communications satellites! This thing could shut down everything—internet, radio, cable, TV. Everything, gone. Like that! This could be the end of the world.

ANDREW: Pictures, do we have pictures?

OLIVER: Not from outer space, no.

ANDREW: Pictures tell the story, Oliver.

OLIVER: This is happening in real time, right now.
ANDREW: No pictures, no story.
OLIVER: We lead with this tonight. This is epic, this is an act of god!
ANDREW: I need you to focus on me.
OLIVER: Are you / listening? … What?!
ANDREW: Oliver, I am desperate. Please! I need help.
OLIVER: Okay. Okay. What is it?
ANDREW: Just now? Just before? … I had an accident.
OLIVER: [*reassuring*] Don't be embarrassed. For a man of your age, accidents are very common, we can clean you up and—
ANDREW: [*raises finger*] An automobile accident and this could get very messy for us.
OLIVER: For us?
ANDREW: I was in the RTN car park. Reversing the Audi. And I hit a Tesla.
OLIVER: Did you hurt anybody?
ANDREW: Not physically, no, but … the driver of the Tesla?
OLIVER: The guy you hit?
ANDREW: Allegedly.
OLIVER: He works here?
ANDREW: No. He *used* to work here but—
OLIVER: You fired him?! Don't … / Please don't tell me you fired him!
ANDREW: No. Just let me tell the story, Christ. No, I didn't fire him … I *employed* him.
OLIVER: Is that better or worse?
ANDREW: He was my first producer, it was a long time ago, and he was great! But then Brian poached him, he spiraled, he got fired and he went to the dark side.
OLIVER: Drugs and alcohol?
ANDREW: Public Relations.
OLIVER: What is he doing here?
ANDREW: I don't know, but Oliver? The actual problem is …

Right at this moment in time, I do not have—

OLIVER: Insurance? You let your / insurance lapse?
ANDREW: Of course, I have insurance. Mate. I'm not a maniac.
OLIVER: What don't you have?
ANDREW: A driver's licence.
OLIVER: Are you fucking kidding me?

ANDREW: Temporary suspension.
OLIVER: / Andrew Carter, no …
ANDREW: Eighteen months. My lawyer cut a deal.
OLIVER: You just had a car crash!
ANDREW: It was a bump, a little car bump.
OLIVER: Are you lying right now? /
ANDREW: Oliver, please shut up and be useful.
OLIVER: What do you need me to do?
ANDREW: It's very simple. I just need *you* to say you were driving my car.
OLIVER: But I wasn't driving your car, Andrew. /
ANDREW: Okay, great! So, *you* tell me who *was* driving my car? Because I don't have a licence, so it *couldn't have been me*. No! This is the story. You picked me up from squash in my Audi, as you often do, and you were parking the car. Simple! Got it?
OLIVER: There are security cameras everywhere.
ANDREW: Video is contestable.
OLIVER: Did he see you behind the wheel?
ANDREW: ChatGPT can put your body on my face.
OLIVER: It doesn't work like that.
ANDREW: I don't care how this works in your head, but I have to be the victim!
OLIVER: You crashed into him. That makes him the victim and you the perpetrator.
ANDREW: Jesus! When did you turn so woke?
OLIVER: I honestly want to help you but you / have to understand …
ANDREW: Get with the program and protect me from any form of responsibility!

If I lose my job, you lose yours.
OLIVER: You wanna be a victim?
ANDREW: Yes! I have / to be a victim!
OLIVER: You want to look like a / victim?!
ANDREW: Yes! Don't just stand there! Help me! I have to be the victim!

OLIVER *dips a sausage roll in tomato sauce and wipes it on* ANDREW*'s ear like a make-up brush.*

OLIVER: Now, you look like a victim.

ANDREW: Really?
OLIVER: Yes. This is what a victim looks like.
ANDREW: Sick. Bring me a mirror.
OLIVER: [*to audience*] But before I can bring him a mirror—
ANDREW: [*to audience*] Out of nowhere!
OLIVER: [*to audience*] He appears.

THREE

PETER *appears in sunglasses, holding a traveller's suit bag, a leather manbag satchel and a disposable coffee cup.*

ANDREW: [*to* PETER] Peter Franger Francis!
PETER: Andrew Carter, you are a crazy man. / Hey? Car-azy. Mate.
ANDREW: You can talk! Hey, hey. Mate! Welcome home.
PETER: Good to see you buddy. God. Look at this place.
ANDREW: Crazy! / Right?
PETER: This is nuts. [*re: the folding table*] We havin' a picnic, what the fuck?
ANDREW: [*cheerful*] Temporary. Ollie, run out to the bar, and get us some drinks.
OLIVER: [*obviously impressed by* PETER*'s presence*] What would you like?
ANDREW: Doubles.
OLIVER: Of what?
ANDREW: Doesn't matter. Just go.
OLIVER: [*to audience*] I tell Andrew to [*To* ANDREW] make good choices.
ANDREW: [*to audience*] And then Oliver disappears.

OLIVER *disappears.*

Peter's phone alerts. Peter reads and types an email while the scene continues.

FOUR

ANDREW: [*to* PETER] I didn't even know you were in the country and there you are, in the RTN car park. What are the odds, right? You know, it's a / funny thing—

PETER: Sorry mate, I've just got to finish—this.

ANDREW: Absolutely. Gotta stay in the loop. Anyway, great to see you.

PETER *laughs at the email he's writing.*

... Something funny?

PETER: [*smiling and typing*] Oh, I just made fifty grand.

ANDREW: Jesus. How'd you do that?

PETER: Like this.

PETER *sends an email and says:*

Whoosh!

ANDREW: Public Relations.

PETER: California Communications has got fifteen full-timers, six sub-contractors and an intern. We dominate crisis management and 'reputational rehabilitation' in the most saturated media landscape in history. Next quarter, I open an office in Austin, Texas. It's a little bit more than 'PR', but shit—What's it been, ten years?

ANDREW: Lost count.

PETER: Lost count, and this is how you live now?

ANDREW: Your skin is translucent.

PETER: I eat a lot of mangoes.

ANDREW: The California climate suits you.

PETER: I am the American dream.

ANDREW: [*laughing*] Which explains why you were driving on the wrong side of the road. I am running to meet a source about a solar storm story, so let's just keep this simple.

He writes a note on a scrap of paper from under whiteboard.

My account. BSB.

He offers it to PETER.

Five K, call it quits. Yep?

PETER: [*smiling*] You want me to transfer you five thousand dollars?

ANDREW: You wanna pay cash—?

PETER: [*smiling*] Just get your people to talk with my insurance company.

ANDREW: Paperwork! Blah! Four grand cash and 'nothing happened here'.

PETER: But something *did* happen here, Andrew, you ran into me.

ANDREW: This kinda feels like a 'shake down'. [*To* OLIVER] Oliver! Where is that alcohol? [*To* PETER] Let's just cut a deal.

PETER: Normal people swap licence details and insurance companies, that's the deal.

ANDREW: Just going to stop you there, Franger.

PETER: Please, don't call me that.

OLIVER *arrives with whiskey and glasses, pours for* PETER *and* ANDREW *while ...*

ANDREW: Best and final, I cover the costs on the Audi, you cover your Tesla.

PETER: That Tesla is a rental … [*re:* ANDREW*'s head*] Is that blood?

ANDREW: Yes. A wound from the accident.

PETER: I did not hit you that hard.

ANDREW: So you *admit* you are at fault?

PETER: Okay! You wanna be an arsehole? Let's all be fucking arseholes!

PETER *slugs back his coffee and presents* ANDREW *with the cup.*

ANDREW: What the fuck is this?

PETER: This is a piss cup.

ANDREW: It's a—what did you say?

PETER: This is a piss cup.

ANDREW: / Are you joking?

OLIVER: Oh my god.

PETER: Super common in California.

ANDREW: You want me to—

PETER: Piss. Yes. Gimme a sample.

ANDREW: Are you seriously going to drug test me in a double almond latte?

PETER: It's just a bit of piss.

ANDREW: Donated via my penis.

PETER: Why are you making this weird?

ANDREW: I am not the one making this / weird, mate.

PETER: We need a sample for the incident report!

ANDREW: Since when do we write incident reports? /

PETER: Standard procedure. /

ANDREW: 'Standard procedure' is for staff. I am still 'on-air talent'!

PETER: So, you refuse to provide a sample?

ANDREW: Good journos never leak!
PETER: You look like a victim.
OLIVER: He is!
PETER: I better call a paramedic.
OLIVER: / No. That's not necessary.
ANDREW: No need to get hysterical / no need for a paramedic!
PETER: [*approaching*] It could be a delayed concussion.
ANDREW: Stand back! Don't touch me!

PETER *wipes his finger in the blood, and examines his finger.*

Don't do that!
OLIVER: [*to audience*] Peter tastes 'the blood' on his finger.

PETER *tastes the 'blood' on his finger.*

PETER: This 'blood' is very salty. /
OLIVER: Wine! They need alcohol! Christine wants Chablis and Leo is doing tequila shots, Brian's party! [*To* ANDREW] If you need me—I am just outside this door.
ANDREW: [*to audience*] And Oliver disappears.

OLIVER *is gone.*

PETER: Ando. What are you doing, mate? You have to take accountability.
ANDREW: Yeah, right.
PETER: 'Accountability' is one of my core values. It will change your life.
ANDREW: Who are you now, fucken Microsoft?
PETER: Mate, you're being very hostile.
ANDREW: Mate! I am a professional journalist, mate! Hostility is my personal brand.
PETER: You need a new mission statement. / Self-loathing is a toxic cycle.
ANDREW: I'm not pissing in that cup! 'Self-loathing'? You sound like a self-help / cult!
PETER: I crawled out of this room with nothing. I was dead and buried in this business, you know that better than anybody. I bought a one-way ticket to the City of Angels, landed with a laptop, a credit card and a URL. Got a shitty apartment in Echo Park, hot desk in Koreatown, instant coffee, instant noodles, and I reinvented my life and look at this place, my god. This place used to be ground zero for news.

Beat. He surveys the room.

Where the fuck are all the flat screens? Used to be CNN, BBC, FOX, and Al Jazeera. Boom. Boom. Boom. Boom. A whole wall of on-air headshots and a trophy cabinet of awards. What the hell is going on?

ANDREW: Awards don't matter.

PETER: Awards are everything.

ANDREW: People vote for their friends.

PETER: That's what losers say.

ANDREW: Journalism is telling stories that some people want to be kept secret. It's not about awards.

PETER: Mate, you know that is bullshit. Journalism is a dead language.

ANDREW: Agree to disagree.

PETER: Awards are the external communication of your commercial value.

ANDREW: I am well aware of my commercial value.

PETER: But you're still here.

ANDREW: Television is my life.

PETER: RTN is a burning building.

ANDREW: It pays the child support.

PETER: Hardwick Holdings is haemorrhaging cash.

ANDREW: I know. / I know that … Yes. It's terrifying.

PETER: Every arm of the business is losing. [*Listing*] Entertainment, factual, movies, sport, / losing, losing, losing, lost.

ANDREW: And Christian Hardwick is dumping all of those losses onto the RTN balance sheet! I know! And, get this! My sources say Hardwick is sending in some consultant to strip-mine us to the bone. They slide in like suicide bombers, pull the pin and boom. Careers go up in smoke!

PETER: Why don't you make a run for it?

ANDREW: Believe me, I would love to, but they need me here, Peter. They want me to stay, and I am a walking ATM for the family. Cindy's lawyers are killing me, Martine wants a Euro-summer-holiday for her fortieth, a bigger house for *her* three kids, now I've got Amy, and Lucas and, shit, what's his name?

PETER: Your producer? /

ANDREW: No. /

PETER: Your bookie? /

ANDREW: Third stepchild. /

PETER: Joshua?

ANDREW: That's it! Fuck! Somedays I wanna roll in here with a semi-automatic and let the shits fall where they may. Obviously, probably not going to do that. But. Is it me or is it suddenly very cold?

PETER: Freezing, like a morgue.

ANDREW: Air-con is schizophrenic, controlled by the Gold Coast office. Tell me if you need a blanket.

PETER: Where is it?

ANDREW: In the blanket cupboard.

PETER: Where is it?

ANDREW: I don't know what you're talking about.

PETER: Andy. We grew up here.

Beat.

ANDREW: Yeah. / Every Wednesday …

PETER: Every Wednesday. You and me and Leo and Colin, pitching stories to the king, and this room was dominated by one giant piece of polished, Indonesian rainforest. And Brian sitting at the head like a pope. Creating us in his own image and I thought I could live with that memory because yes, he was a monster, but monsters are reliable, right? Monsters never change.

Beat.

But, here I am again, and there is a gap in this room. I have to know. Where is it? What happened to the Slab?

ANDREW: [*smiling*] It's actually a funny story …

PETER: All ears.

ANDREW: This one stays in the vault?

PETER: You know me. I throw away the key.

ANDREW *smiles, they share the whiskey, and he shares the story.*

ANDREW: Election night, total disaster. Seat, after seat, after seat and we are trapped in here with Brian, and he cannot believe what is happening. He has spent a lifetime twisting arms and terrorising and look at this fucking landslide. He is taking this loss very personally, and then, when the size of the swing is apparent, Fuck-Knuckle comes out to make his concession speech. Shit gets fucking messy. Brian is full of coke and prosecco, and jumps up on the Slab, screaming at the TV! '*You fucking pissants couldn't lead a conga line! Never surrender!*' And he starts ripping the TVs off the wall, chucking bottles, smashing furniture, and then gets up on the Slab, drops his strides and takes the biggest dump you have ever seen. Roadhouse size. A lifetime of toxicity. Flooooo-p, and it stank like Chernobyl burning rats and he screams, '*I am Brian Mathews! Welcome to this truth.*'

And then he rips all the headshots off the wall, all of the on-air talent, and he smears every face with feces, '*After all I did for you, you backstabbing bastard weak-kneed poofters.*'

Then he falls over backwards. Chauffeur home. Next day, not a word. Back to work. I wish I had his agent. His contract must be more watertight than a blue whale's butthole.

They are both laughing hysterically now, wheezing for breath.

PETER: If you can get away with that, you can get away with anything.

ANDREW: As we speak, the Slab is undergoing industrial steam cleaning, sanding and restaining, costing Christian a fortune, all because Bri-Bri does not do losing well.

PETER: Oh, that's gold. I gotta use that in my speech.

ANDREW: What speech?

PETER: I'm making a speech, for Brian tonight.

ANDREW: *You're* making a speech for Brian Mathews.

PETER: That's right

ANDREW: That story is in the vault. / We agreed.

PETER: No, yeah, yeah. / You're right.

ANDREW: Why the fuck are you making a speech for that prick?

PETER: Fifty years in media.

ANDREW: So what?

PETER: Big-ups. Hey. Who does your socials?

ANDREW: Oliver. My producer.

PETER: Can I borrow him?

ANDREW: He's not a Vespa.

PETER: Can he be trusted?

ANDREW: What kind of a question is that?

PETER: You take control of your own successes.

Lights go to half.

What the fuck?

ANDREW: 'Efficiency'. If nobody moves, the lights assume we're dead.

ANDREW *claps above his head. Lights reinstate.*

If we burst into a round of applause, we could black-out half the neighbourhood … Can we come to a car-crash / agreement?

PETER: No! Stop! For Chrissakes. This is not a negotiation.

PETER *moves to whiteboard, drawing an aerial map of the car park collision.*

This is the RTN car park.

ANDREW: And what is that?

PETER: This is me.

ANDREW: You're very small and flat.

PETER: *This* represents me in my Tesla. *This* is your shitbox Audi. /

ANDREW: 'Shitbox'? … / Did you really just say … 'shitbox' … ?

PETER: You hit the gas instead of the brake. You are not the victim.

PETER *takes a photograph of the whiteboard.*

ANDREW: Okay!

He takes the pen.

Gird your loins, Picasso! *This* is the *Audi* which I drive. And *this* ...

He draws a long awkward shape.

… is your penis substitute.

PETER: That is a Tesla, Model S Plaid! / Zero to a hundred in two point one!

ANDREW: Brian's Merc is *here*! Katie's Lexus, and *this* …

ANDREW *draws a very large square.*

PETER: What the fuck is that?

ANDREW: This is Caroline's Hummer.

PETER: You're a different man.

ANDREW: Peter! I have something to confess.

PETER: Please, don't do that. / Don't do it! Don't do it!

ANDREW: Mate! It is eating me alive, listen! … I do not have a driver's licence.

PETER: Are you serious or are you bullshitting me?

ANDREW: I wish I was. But that shitbox is still registered to my first ex-wife, Cindy. And Martine doesn't know. I can lose my job, I can go to jail! Peter, please. I need help.

PETER: What do you need from me?

ANDREW: Just a little tiny …

PETER: I'm back in the country less than twenty-four hours, and he wants me to lie, for him.

ANDREW: —For my current wife, and my stepchildren, Amy, Lucas and …

PETER: Joshua. /

ANDREW: Insurance fraud is a victimless crime.

PETER: How do we explain the crash?

ANDREW: We keep it simple.

PETER: But what do we say?

ANDREW: May I suggest … 'An act of god'.

PETER: An act of god, in the RTN car park?

ANDREW: A flood, a fire, a magnetic storm.

PETER: An 'act of god'?

ANDREW: The language of the oppressors.

PETER: You haven't changed a bit.

ANDREW: Frank made me get me blonde tips and then he shifted me to late night.

PETER: I saw that. Martine must be pissed.

ANDREW: What do you mean, you 'saw that'?

PETER: Listen, don't worry about the crash. I'll take care of it. For old time's sake.

ANDREW: What is it going to cost me?

PETER: Don't ask any questions and lend me your producer for the weekend. Deal?

They shake hands.

ANDREW: Done. Oliver?!

FIVE

OLIVER: [*to audience*] I meet Ando in the airlock. [*To* ANDREW] What's going on?

ANDREW: I don't know, but nobody flies across the globe to make a speech for Brian.

OLIVER: What did he say about the accident?

ANDREW: He said he's got my back; he said he's taking care of everything.

OLIVER: Really?
ANDREW: [*unsure*] That's what he said.
OLIVER: That's great!
ANDREW: I know!
OLIVER: Okay. So, what do you need from me?
ANDREW: Get in there, be useful, follow his directives, and whatever you do, don't let *that bastard* out of your sight.
OLIVER: Wait a second, where are you going?
ANDREW: The Butcher. I have to get the facts from Frank.
OLIVER: [*to audience*] And Andrew disappears.

ANDREW *disappears.*

SIX

Music. PETER *is alone. Tries on a boxing glove. He moves around this familiar space. Picks up the dumbbell with his gloved hand, he smiles at the effort. It's too heavy. He settles the weight back down, and as the music begins to fade ...*

PETER: [*to audience*] Last time I was in this room, was my last day working for Brian. He sent a message. A demand. I arrived, on time.

OLIVER *appears and watches* PETER *from a distance.*

I waited. Here. And then, when he appeared in the doorway, behind me.

PETER *looks around and stares at* OLIVER.

OLIVER: Sausage roll? …
PETER: No. Thanks.
OLIVER: I just wanted to say, Mr Francis …

Produces a copy of Hollywood Hitman.

Loved it. It is an honour to meet you. Could you? Would you, mind?
PETER: [*re:* OLIVER*'s hat*] 'Unfiltered.' That you?
OLIVER: What? Oh, no. Andrew. His show is, *Andrew Carter: Unfiltered.*
PETER: Is that right?
OLIVER: Do you like it?
PETER: [*preparing to autograph the book*] What'd you say your name is?
OLIVER: Madison. Oliver Madison.

OLIVER: Thank you so much. It's sick. Obviously, I have notes but, oh! Can you make it out to 'Jasmine'?

PETER: You don't look like a 'Jasmine'.

OLIVER: We do a podcast together.

PETER: Jasmine?

OLIVER: She's super scrappy. PA to the Director of News.

PETER: Frank Butcher?

OLIVER: Have you met Frank?

PETER: Yup. [*Signing*] So, what's your podcast about?

OLIVER: Media, culture and UFOs. We use the voice-over studio after hours. Is it true Netflix optioned your life rights?

PETER: [*flattered*] It's just an option.

OLIVER: Soo great. Would you like to guest on our pod?

PETER closes the book, holds it out. OLIVER goes to take it, but PETER holds it.

PETER: Okay. Are you serious?

OLIVER: About the guesting? Yes.

PETER: No. You have 'notes' on my memoir?

OLIVER: Yeah. Sure. Bit obsessed.

PETER: It's a bestseller.

OLIVER: It should be.

PETER: It is. Andrew says you do all his socials.

OLIVER: I do.

PETER: I need some specific hashtags on the RTN feeds.

OLIVER: What for?

PETER: To highlight Brian Mathews. Fifty years in media.

OLIVER: Everybody's got a Brian story.

PETER: I want all eyes on Brian tonight.

OLIVER: You don't need hashtags to do that.

PETER: I know what I want, mate.

OLIVER: Hashtags are obsolete. They waste a lot of characters.

PETER: I don't think you understand the direction.

OLIVER: With respect, I think I do. You want to corral the stories around Brain, 'the man, the myth, the defamation action.' Well, the algorithm does that for you.

I can draw up a strategy if that helps.

PETER: I don't need a strategy; I am telling you want I want.

OLIVER: With respect, you may not understand the new media / landscape—

PETER: Okay! With respect, just fucking … What are they?

OLIVER: What are hashtags?

PETER: Your notes. On my book.

OLIVER: Notes can be super subjective.

PETER: Spit 'em out.

OLIVER: Are you sure you want my opinion? /

PETER: Cut the crap and tell me, what is wrong with my life?

OLIVER *accepts the challenge and uses the whiteboard to illustrate the notes.*

OLIVER: Okay! First three chapters, slay. You arrive in LA with nothing, instant noodles, instant coffee, and we want you to succeed, we ride with you through the crazy parties and the brand building and the Russian gangsters and then there is this chapter out of nowhere, about your mental breakdown. And we don't know why or what's going on. No explanation. A gap.

PETER: That's how it happens.

OLIVER: Well, I don't buy it.

PETER: You don't buy my mental breakdown?

OLIVER: Feels like a trope.

PETER: A trope?

OLIVER: It slows the story engine. Be honest, Peter. *Hollywood Hitman*?

The title screams: 'sex and drugs and—crisis management!' We want the hitman to name the names, count the bodies, attack, attack, come on. Nobody is reading this book for a whole chapter of 'Poor, poor me.'

PETER: I was diagnosed with PTSD.

OLIVER: Okay, from what?

Beat.

See, I paid thirty-five dollars for your life story. /

PETER: And the *Guardian* fucking loved it!

OLIVER: / Okay—

PETER: The *New York* fucking *Times*, the *LA Times*! The *Economist* called it 'a triumph' and Netflix want a returnable series.

OLIVER: It's good. But it could've been great.

Beat.

PETER: Go get started on the hashtags.

OLIVER: But I thought I told you, / hashtags are obsolete.

PETER: When I was your age, we took fucking orders, or we suffered the consequences, we did what we were told to do, and we knew when to shut the fuck up! We didn't wear hats to work, we were journalists!

Silence. Then he recalibrates his attitude.

Not cool. I have values. This place …

I know this can be a difficult place to work.

OLIVER: How do you know that?

PETER: Take my advice: get out. I am sorry, I hurt your feelings.

OLIVER: Feelings are for children and the mentally weak.

Beat. PETER *is impressed.*

[*To audience*] Then he says—

PETER: Okay, kid. Do you wanna see me make a hundred grand?

OLIVER: [*to audience*] And I reply, [*To* PETER] Yes, please, I would love that.

PETER *shows an email on his phone to* OLIVER. *Cue music. They pick up STORY mics.*

PETER: [*announcing like an MC at the UFC*] New client for California Communications. Record producer. You know him. Now, listen to this: 'Hi Pete, I know you're super busy. But can you please draft a statement for "Client's Name". Urgent.' Scroll to the facts:

OLIVER: [*on mic*] 'Ten hours ago, "Client's Name" took a whole bunch of cocaine, Viagra, mushrooms and mescaline. Goes out with the entourage and starts bro-posting about "Sometimes your bitch needs a slap" and a bunch of 'Hitler' shit, wakes up naked, under a bridge, beats up a homeless person, has sex with a tree and gets arrested.' [*To* PETER] 'Client's Name' had sex with a tree?

PETER: That's what it says!

OLIVER: This is a career-ending story.

PETER: That's why they came to me. They need a strategy.

So, what do we do about this?

OLIVER: I would love to know. What do you do?

PETER: Grasshopper. I write an email.

'On behalf of our client, we would like to address the recent incident that has garnered attention. "Client's Name" deeply regrets any distress or concern. The events were the result of a lapse in judgment that do not reflect his true values, and we ask the public and the media to … ' [*To* OLIVER] What do we want the media to do?

OLIVER: 'Refrain from rushing to judgment before the facts are established!'

PETER: Love it.

OLIVER: 'The statements on social media do not align with his values, and we are investigating a potential hacking event.' /

PETER: 'This is a pivotal moment for personal growth.'

OLIVER: 'We will provide further updates as appropriate.'

PETER: 'And we ask that all media outlets respect "Client's Name's" privacy!

As he navigates this process.' Send to all contacts!

BOTH: Whoosh!

PETER *and* OLIVER *are elated.*

OLIVER: Hectic! I don't even vape, but I would murder a cigarette right now.

PETER: [*smiling*] You're a natural-born killer, kid.

OLIVER: Well, I do like making shit up.

PETER: The world is out there. What's stopping you, are you married?

OLIVER: I live with my parents.

PETER: Are you married to your parents?

OLIVER: I'm living with my parents to save enough money, so I don't have to live on cat food when I get a place of my / own and …

PETER: That's not a plan, that is a nightmare.

OLIVER: Andrew has got great connections; he is really trying to help me.

PETER: Ando is a dinosaur.

OLIVER: But this is what you did, right? This is where it all started for you.

PETER: So, what do you want after RTN?

OLIVER: I want Netflix to option my life rights. [*To audience*] Then he says—

PETER: My assistant Bianca is back in LA. I need somebody who can—

OLIVER: [*to audience*] 'Deep-dive contracts, work as directed.'
PETER: [*to* OLIVER] This could be the opportunity of a lifetime.
OLIVER: [*to audience*] And so I say, [*To* PETER] Where do I sign?

PETER *gives* OLIVER *an iPad.*

PETER: [*to audience*] It's a non-disclosure agreement.
OLIVER: [*to audience*] The RTN standard contract has got a confidentiality clause—
PETER: You are reporting to me directly. Crisis management. Lose the hat.
OLIVER: Okay. / Got it.
PETER: This is a newsroom, not a dive bar, and keep these things away from me.

He tosses OLIVER *a pack of Marlboros.*

I have to give up again.
OLIVER: Okay. And the rest.

Beat.

Come on.

Beat. PETER *reaches into his jacket pocket, pulls out a pack of smokes.*

And the rest.

Beat.

You've got a spare pack in your sock.

Beat. PETER, *reaches into his boot and pulls out a pack of cigarettes.*

PETER: Bianca doesn't know about the sock.

He tosses the cigarettes to OLIVER.

OLIVER: Bianca hasn't read *Hollywood Hitman*.
PETER: I need headshots of all the on-air talent, and a bag of Pink Ladies.
OLIVER: You want headshots and apples?
PETER: Mastication kills the pain. And tell me when it's time for my speech.
Set an alarm, don't fuck it up.
OLIVER: Roger that. [*To audience*] I exit, and I meet Andrew in the airlock and—

SEVEN

ANDREW: He's not in the studio, he's not in his office, he's not at the fucking party! Nobody knows where Frank Butcher is, and people do not just disappear!

OLIVER: You do all the time.

ANDREW: I am not the Director of News, but I am a 'nominee'!

I just got myself nominated for the West Southeast Asia Domestic International Media and Communications Awards and Prizes.

OLIVER: Is that a fucking thing?

ANDREW: / Jump on their website, get me into the public domain.

OLIVER: [*googling them on his phone*] Oh god, an alert, the geomagnetic storm; 'Early warnings of low-earth-orbit satellite failures'. /

ANDREW: Yes, yes, do you see my name in the Google?

OLIVER: Did you hear what I said about the end of the world?

ANDREW: You *are* still Googling the / West Southeast Asia Domestic International Media and Communications Awards and Prizes, right?

OLIVER: Yes I am, but Andrew, this Award is a total scam! Categories include [*Reading*] 'Best Infomercial, English-speaking. Best Voice-Over for Tobacco Advertising, in multiple languages.'

ANDREW: Mine is 'Body of Work', you can / search by my name—

OLIVER: You paid a 'nomination fee'!

ANDREW: It's an administrative deposit!

OLIVER: Non-refundable five thousand / dollars.

ANDREW: But they engrave your name on the trophy!

OLIVER: And you have to collect it 'in person' and 'stay at a partner hotel'.

Andrew, what the fuck? This is humiliating, for both of us!

ANDREW: Awards are the external communication of success.

OLIVER: The geomagnetic storm could be an actual award-winning story and …

ANDREW: / I think Peter Francis is the consultant!

OLIVER: I think Peter Francis is the consultant!

ANDREW: / What makes you think Peter Francis is the consultant?

OLIVER: What makes you think Peter Francis is the consultant?

ANDREW: / He is a crisis management expert!

OLIVER: He is a crisis management expert and Netflix optioned his life rights.

ANDREW: *And* he is 'making a speech for Brian' tonight! /

OLIVER: *And* he made me sign an NDA, / but apart from that?

ANDREW: But apart from that? It's just a hunch. Jesus, Oliver, what do we do?!

OLIVER: You get your arse in there, get up in his grill and don't take any shit and whatever you do: do not let him out of your sight! Got it?

ANDREW: Got it! [*To audience*] And Oliver disappears.

OLIVER *disappears.*

EIGHT

ANDREW: [*to audience*] My mind is a madness. Are we right? Are we wrong?

Oliver signed an NDA? … Netflix own the rights to Franger's life? …

Is Peter really the consultant? Fuck. I gave him his first job in this business and now, is he coming for me? I am in contortion. Compose myself.

He closes his eyes and deep breathing.

Deep breath, into the chakra.

He has a coughing fit.

Right down into the ying and the yang. I am responsible for my own failures and my own successes. Yesses. To paraphrase Winston Churchill, 'When you enter an ambush meeting it's wise to bring good news about you,' or something like that.

He opens his eyes.

And with this positive energy in my veins, I am propelled into the conference room. And this is how that begins!

NINE

ANDREW *is propelled into the conference room.*

ANDREW: Amazing news about me! I have been nominated! *Finally!*

PETER: A Walkley?

ANDREW: So much better! The West Southeast Asia Domestic *International* Media and Communications Awards and Prizes. It's a very big deal, a great honour, and an authentic, real, award.

He smiles.

So, I am a journalist of value, and Oliver tells / me—

PETER: Oliver signed an NDA.

ANDREW: Not worth the iPad it's written on, is it? Don't get me wrong, it's good to see you. We go back to the Big Bang. But mano to mano, direct question. Should anybody in this room be feeling nervous? Yes or no. Are you / the—

PETER: [*can't contain his excitement*] Yes. Andrew. I am the consultant.

ANDREW: Fuck me swinging, are you're kidding? / I knew it! I guessed that! … Yes.

PETER: I'm only going to say this once. Shut up and listen. This is confidential!

Beat.

Christian Hardwick has hired me to gut Real Time News. He wants a fifty-percent cut of salary expenditure *across the board*. I've got forty-eight hours to reorganise the entire roster. If he likes it?

Thumbs up.

If he hates it, I'm on the first flight home.

ANDREW: Christian hired you personally.

PETER: Yes.

ANDREW: [*to audience*] Okay. Christian is chair of the board. Forget what I said, about consultants being evil … This could be good for me. [*To* PETER] Why did he come to you personally?

PETER: Cali Comms helped him out when he had a little 'trouble in Russia'.

ANDREW: I didn't know he had any 'trouble in Russia'.

PETER: [*smiling*] Exactly.

They laugh conspiratorially.

By the end of tonight, these walls will be dripping in blood, and you cannot breathe a word about this. If the market finds out I am here, the share price is going to tank.

ANDREW: No! The market will love you! You're a prodigal son, forsaking your Cali Comms to come and cauterise the festering wound of RTN. Give this newsman a round of applause!

ANDREW *starts applauding ... the lights go out!*

PETER: Mate. I am not walking away from Cali Comms. I can multitask.

PETER *claps his hands above his head and lights reinstate.*

ANDREW: But. Do you think that's …

PETER: Possible?

ANDREW: Ethical.

PETER: 'Ethical' is a word, and since moving to the States, I am a very visual person.

ANDREW: But journalists work by a code of ethics.

PETER: What is a journalist, right? I write bestsellers.

ANDREW: So, you think you can run a TV news channel *and* be CEO of a public relations company at the same time.

PETER: What's wrong with that?

ANDREW: It's a conflict of interest. Butcher will never accept it.

PETER: Forget about Frank Butcher.

ANDREW: But Frank is Director of News.

PETER: He was, but Frank is gone.

ANDREW: Frank is / gone?

PETER: Frank is not coming back. For good.

ANDREW: … because of me?

PETER: Not everything is about you.

ANDREW: Agree to disagree. /

PETER: Frank was a problem and so now, Frank is gone.

ANDREW: Peter, did you have Frank murdered?

PETER: Transferred to the Gold Coast.

ANDREW: [*pure shock*] Holy Jesus …

PETER: I tried to work with Frank. But Frank is a relic, Andrew. A man who walks in the street and doesn't know where he's going. A melon, a deadweight smothering, an anvil on a puppy. Frank Butcher has the vision of a fence post, the instinct of a lemming and the intellect of fruit. The on-air roster he left behind reads like a fucking friendship bracelet. In my professional opinion, Frank Butcher is a waste of DNA. But I know he's a good friend of yours.

ANDREW: No, no … Butcher is no friend of mine, / no …

PETER: You sure about that?

ANDREW: Much closer to enemies in my estimation. No, this place is a palace of lies. You know what you need? You need a two IC. Somebody you can trust. You need an inside man, to help you navigate the facts from the truth. You *know* you can trust me. We know where the bodies are buried.

They laugh together.

PETER: No.

ANDREW: Franger, you owe me one.

PETER: Andrew. / No.

ANDREW: Who gave you your first job?

PETER: Brian.

ANDREW: You bloody liar, Franger. No. / You know you owe me.

PETER: Do not call me that bloody / name. I'm not joking.

ANDREW: 'Franger' is a term of endearment! Who gave you your first job?

OLIVER *appears with headshots and an apple.*

PETER: Brian Mathews hired me! / You know that!

ANDREW: I was producing for Brian, and / you were …

PETER: Brian hired *me*, and you have never gotten over it.

ANDREW: He didn't even know you were alive!

PETER: He was looking for future on-air talent.

ANDREW: And how did that work out for you?

OLIVER: Headshots as requested.

PETER: [*to* OLIVER] Is it time for my speech?

OLIVER: Not yet.

PETER: Brian trending?

OLIVER: Not trending, but we have garnered some meaningful engagement.

PETER: What are people saying about him?

OLIVER: A random sample of replies; 'What *is* truth in a post-fake-news world? … Can truth coexist with fact, anymore? Is truth a twentieth-century construct, outdated and outmoded by impressions, and engagement?'

PETER: What the fuck is that?

OLIVER: A pretty interesting hot take.

ANDREW: Are you running a campaign for Brian?

PETER: What hashtag did you throw up?

OLIVER: 'Hashtag Welcome to the Truth.'

PETER: The hashtag for Brian's fiftieth anniversary is 'Hashtag Welcome to the Truth'?

OLIVER: Do you love it?

PETER: No! *And* I have notes.

ANDREW: 'Welcome to the Truth' is the Hindenburg of hashtags.

OLIVER: But he starts every show with 'I am Brian Mathews. Welcome to the Truth.'

It's his classic opening line—

PETER: I know it is, I wrote it. It's a contract with an audience.

ANDREW: But it makes for a shithouse hashtag.

OLIVER: There is nothing wrong with the truth.

ANDREW: It buries the bloody lede.

OLIVER: A hashtag does not have a / lede, it is just a fucking hashtag.

ANDREW: / Agree to disagree.

PETER: Agree to disagree! It carries your banner into the battle! 'Hashtag It's My Party! Hashtag BrianFifty, Hashtag BriBri'. /

OLIVER: 'Hashtag Welcome to the Truth'!

PETER: Is pompous and bewildering.

ANDREW: Like reading *Mein Kampf* on the beach.

PETER: You're supposed to understand this shit, writing is editing, boy!

OLIVER: … Andrew?

Moment.

ANDREW: Very disappointing.

OLIVER: [*a level-headed rage*] Okay! I get it. Sick! These are the heads you wanted!

He slaps the magnetic headshots onto the table.

[*To audience on mic*] I am working as directed, attending to *notes* on a hashtag. Right through that wall at Brian's party, canapés are cavorting with champagne, the prawns are on the pole but in the skies above our heads, an entire fleet of low-orbit satellites has just dropped out of sync! The sky in this business is literally falling, but we don't have any pictures, so we're ignoring the coming devastation! Instead, inside the conference room the Hitman lays out his targets. Headshots.

PETER *is laying the headshots out on the floor like a crime scene.*

ANDREW: [*to audience on mic*] My colleagues, my comrades, my competition.

OLIVER: [*to audience*] This is kill or be killed.

ANDREW: [*to audience*] And like a lover's final breath … I refuse to look away.

OLIVER *disappears.*

TEN

ANDREW *joins* PETER.

ANDREW: The kid reminds me of a younger me.

PETER: The impotent rage.

ANDREW: The howl in a mirror. Epic.

They survey the headshots together, like detectives at a murder scene.

This is quite a hit list.

PETER: This is not a 'hit list'.

ANDREW: It looks like a hit list.

PETER: This is a reorganisational mood board, with extreme prejudice.
We start with the daylight shift. Clinical review. Okay?

ANDREW: Mate. Some of these people have families.
Renee has got a daughter and a car loan and …

PETER: But what do we *think* of Renee?

PETER *slaps her headshot on the whiteboard.*

ANDREW *makes a decision to try and save some of his colleagues.*

ANDREW: Renee's great.

ANDREW removes her headshot to the safety of the table.

All over the brief. Six a.m. to nine a.m., *News World* is a solid start.

PETER: Then, *Capital Morning*.

PETER slaps Eleni's headshot on the whiteboard.

ANDREW: From nine to twelve.

PETER: What do we think of *Capital Morning*?

ANDREW removes Eleni's headshot to the safety of the table.

ANDREW: Eleni is a pro. And then *Lunch Hour* with John and Michelle, super-smart, great team and excellent coverage and then our afternoon run home is good. Tom and Gary are story-breakers. They set the agenda, every week. If I am being honest? I have to say, our six-to-seven weekdays is very strong.

PETER: But then the sun goes down and the cray-cray comes to play.

ANDREW: Let's not forget, journos need jobs.

PETER: Christian Hardwick wants me to re-woke the news.

ANDREW: Sorry. He wants you to fucking—what did you say?

PETER: He wants me to re-woke the news.

ANDREW: Is that a thing?

PETER: It is to him.

ANDREW: He wants more woke or less?

PETER: More. Lot more. The election result was a wake-up call. The ratings are in the toilet. He wants to steer this ship in a new direction.

ANDREW: But … we are the conservative voice of outrage.

PETER: The future is multi-platform. Podcasts, interactives. New voices.

ANDREW: Is this about me?

PETER: No.

ANDREW: I feel I am being blamed.

PETER: I am telling you what Christian Hardwick, chair of the board, wants me to do. There aren't enough Boomers to keep RTN alive, this is generational change. We go woke or we go broke. Half the roster is getting cut. This is happening, tonight. Mate, I've got your back on the car crash. Are you with me, or are you against me?

A ticking noise.

ELEVEN

ANDREW: [*to audience on mic*] Welcome to the night of the long whiteboard markers. We debate the pros and cons. *Everybody* is on the table. What do we think of Christine Spencer? [*To* PETER] She's smart, great contacts, but …

PETER: Okay! She's gone. Next!

ANDREW: [*to audience*] I am freezing, and I feel sick.

> PETER *places the headshot on the whiteboard, draws a circle around it.*

[*To audience*] And this is when it is very clear, if I am going to save my skin, I need more than a fake award, I need to roll a couple of corpses out into the path of the fucking freight train. [*To* PETER] Got one! Colin! What do we think of Colin?

> ANDREW *re-enters conference room, lays the STORY mic on the table, and picks up Colin's headshot.*

PETER: Yes, good old Colin. What do we think of Colin?

ANDREW: The man is a mental black hole. At last year's Christmas party, he photocopied his left foot. Not his bum. That man is not right in the head.

> ANDREW *slaps Colin onto the whiteboard.*

> OLIVER *enters with an iPad.*

OLIVER: I updated / the hashtags to reflect your intentions—

ANDREW: Mate, I am right in the middle of murdering Colin.

OLIVER: [*holding the iPad for* ANDREW] I think you need to read this!

PETER: Is it time for my speech?

OLIVER: Not yet. [*To* ANDREW] Satellites are in free fall.

PETER: Is Brian Mathews trending?

OLIVER: No. But 'fascist shill' is getting good engagement / and—

ANDREW: Why are we throwing this prick a party?

OLIVER: Because he always wins his first five minutes, and outrage gets the clicks.

PETER: Exactly. /

ANDREW: The first five minutes are easy.

OLIVER: / Andrew … Andrew! … Andrew!!

ANDREW: An hysterical personal attack. Anyone can / win the first five. But what happens after that?

OLIVER: I need you to read the copy I wrote for the satellite story, / data.

PETER: Actually! Oliver! Yes!

OLIVER: Me?

PETER: Take a seat.

OLIVER: / Me? Are you sure? …

PETER: You are the demographic; I need you in here. [*To* ANDREW, *re:* OLIVER] This is the algorithm.

He picks up the STORY mic and turns to OLIVER.

Now. Ollie? Safe space. Don't be shy, my boy. This is a directive. What do we think of Colin?

PETER *uses the mic like a reporter, amplifying questions and answers.*

OLIVER: [*to audience*] I don't know what that means.

PETER: Does Colin resonate with new audiences?

OLIVER: [*to audience*] And I don't know what that / means.

PETER: Get on the Slab and pitch, boy!

OLIVER: [*to audience*] And I really don't know what that means.

PETER: This is your chance to impress! Give me your opinion. Ready, set, go!

OLIVER: [*to audience*] I don't know what he wants to hear and so I take a chance, and I tell him the truth. [*To* PETER, *on mic*] Colin is posting cat videos and that is *in*appropriate content.

ANDREW: Colin is posting cat videos?

OLIVER: [*on mic*] Fuck yes.

ANDREW: Actual cats on video?

OLIVER: [*on mic*] Yes. On RTN socials and I think that is unprofessional.

ANDREW: That Colin is one loose unit.

PETER: [*on mic*] Colin can be terminated.

ANDREW: Agree to agree.

PETER: Oliver! Email Colin. 'Contract terminated, for being a cat-vid-posting freak.

OLIVER: [*to audience*] And this is when I start recording.

He openly places his recorder in the middle of the table.

I will take notes, but audio helps me transcribe.

PETER: Good boy.

OLIVER: And Colin is terminated for what 'specific reason'?

PETER: Incorrect use of social media.

ANDREW: And that 'foot on the photocopier' shit.

OLIVER: [*to* ANDREW *specifically*] And this is why you're ending his career?

ANDREW: … We're not putting him to sleep. He'll go live on a farm in the country.

Get a late-night slot on regional radio, quizzes and book reviews.

PETER: He'll be happier with his own kind.

ANDREW: Besides, without all that make-up, he looks like a deep-fried sock.

OLIVER: But for the record, you're literally firing him for posting cats?

PETER: Yes. And thank you for bringing his thought crime to my attention.

'Leo!'

Looks to ANDREW.

What do we think of Leo?

ANDREW *picks up Leo's headshot. Beat. He commits.*

ANDREW: All butter, no bread. Should be arrested for impersonating a / personality.

PETER: He started the same week as me and he's still hanging around, like a wire coat hanger from the dry cleaner's, clingy plastic, nothing inside.

ANDREW: [*into recorder*] Are we worried about his ketamine habit?

PETER: His fucken what?

ANDREW: Bigtime on the gear.

PETER: I worked with him for years and he never once offered me a line.

ANDREW: [*into recorder*] The filthy keta-hoarder-prick!

PETER: Oliver! Note! [*Into recorder*] Piss test the special-K junkie!

PETER *and* ANDREW *laugh.*

ANDREW: To the Gold Coast Gulag.

He places Leo on the board and writes 'Gulag'.

PETER: [*surprised and impressed*] Next!

ANDREW: What do we think about Caroline? /

PETER: / Caroline!

ANDREW: Sweet Caroline!

ANDREW *picks up Caroline's headshot.*

PETER: She does have a bit of a horse face.

ANDREW: Classic 'Sigourney' droop. Like a palsy.

PETER: But attractive.

ANDREW: What?

PETER: Useful elongation. Great for TikTok and split screen.

OLIVER: Brian is a big fan of Caroline. /

PETER: Is Caroline a big fan of Brian?

OLIVER: They hang on weekends. He says she 'oozes' integrity.

ANDREW: Ghastly.

OLIVER: See her interview with Fuck-Knuckle? You could build a roster around her.

ANDREW: Steady on.

OLIVER: Her bio is to die for.

ANDREW: Padded, completely / padded. Caroline doesn't go close to woke.

OLIVER: Former Chief of Staff for Immigration and Border Force, she looks like she's been to war and seen some awful fucking shit.

ANDREW: Has she been nominated for any awards, recently?

OLIVER: She is out there at the party right now, I can bring her in and ask her?

ANDREW: No! No! / No, cool your jets, mate.

Slaps Caroline's headshot on the board.

PETER: No need, no. Oliver. Note: new hair, personal trainer, lose five Ks.

OLIVER: Is this for me?

ANDREW *writes 'lose weight'.*

PETER: For Caroline. If she does that, she can stay, otherwise? Boot! Next.

ANDREW: [*picking up the next headshot*] Next on the list is Stanley / Monroe.

OLIVER: Stanley / Monroe.

ANDREW: Okay! *This guy* is a fucking stiff.

OLIVER: 'Expert in financial transitioning of Asian economies.'
ANDREW: I mean, what is that? Some kind of street / food?
PETER: He looks like a pervert's mugshot.
ANDREW: He is a 1982 weirdo.
PETER: What's he got left on his contract?
OLIVER: [*checking on the iPad*] His contract? What does that matter?
PETER: If he's out of contract, I can just drop him. No payout. Nothing.
ANDREW: No payout?
OLIVER: [*reading contract deets off the iPad*] Three years left to run.

ANDREW *is astonished Stanley has this much time left.*

ANDREW: Three years? Wow.
PETER: Fucken unions.
ANDREW: Wo-ow. /
OLIVER: He came from the *Canberra Standard*, they are sooo legacy media.
ANDREW: / Just. Wow.
PETER: Three years is going to be way too expensive.
ANDREW: Three years? / Wow!
PETER: Okay! Oliver! We write an email. To: Stanley Monroe.
OLIVER: [*to audience*] Here we go.
PETER: Subject: Formal Notification of Employment Status and Pending Investigation. Following recent developments this is to formally notify you of immediate changes to your employment status. Effective immediately, you will be stood down from all on-air duties. An internal investigation is being convened into reports of your conduct wholly inconsistent with RTN's code of ethics and standards. Pending the outcome of this process, you are being reassigned to … 'Special Projects'.
ANDREW: What the hell is 'Special Projects'?
PETER: A non-operational placement.

At this point, two outcomes are available to you:

A managed exit arrangement consisting of a 'farewell week', followed by a severance package equivalent to six weeks' salary.

Alternatively, you may elect to be held to the terms of your existing contract, during which time you will remain suspended, under investigation, with no active duties or public profile.

Signed. Fuck you, from me.

ANDREW: [*applauding*] That is a work of art! A fucking professional hit. 'Assigned to Special Projects.' [*Into recorder*] He just made that up!

OLIVER: You're going to pay Stan to sit in the office and do nothing for the rest of his contract.

PETER: No way, that cunt's in the car park.

ANDREW *and* PETER *are laughing as the scene continues,* ANDREW *slaps Stanley's headshot on the board, and noting 'car park'.*

Thank you for your service, Stanley.

OLIVER: We need to bring HR and legal into this.

ANDREW: No! No. HR don't work / this late.

PETER: [*on mic*] No, I don't think Legal need to be here.

OLIVER: I am just voicing a strategic concern / that—

PETER: [*on mic*] You signed an NDA, my boy. Next on the list, is? …

OLIVER: Next on the list is …

OLIVER *and* ANDREW *exchange a look. It is Andrew.* OLIVER *initiates the action, picks up the last remaining headshot, with a faux smile.*

Andrew Carter…

He puts Andrew's headshot on the board.

ANDREW: [*joining in with laughter*] Andrew bloody Carter!

PETER: I cannot believe he's still here! / Right?

ANDREW: Veteran reporter. Ruggedly handsome.

PETER: [*makes a buzzer noise*] Move him on! Get him outta here!

ANDREW: [*joking*] Get rid of him! Exterminate! Exterminate!

PETER: His ratings are in the toilet!

ANDREW: Fucking terrible!

PETER: A pompous, aging, potted plant!

ANDREW: [*taking his headshot down*] In his defence. Frank gave him a shithouse timeslot.

PETER: Sounds like an excuse.

ANDREW: Is this a joke? I thought we were joking. Yes?

OLIVER: [*to audience*] Andrew's phone is ringing.

ANDREW *looks to* OLIVER. *Holds his stare.*

ANDREW: I need to take this call … Two minutes.

ANDREW *places his headshot on the table.*

PETER: Everything in this room is classified information.
ANDREW: Absolutely, absolutely. One second.

ANDREW *is exiting whilst answering the phone.*

[*On phone*] Hey. You got my message?

We hear some party music starting from the party for Brian next door.

TWELVE

OLIVER: How deep are you cutting?
PETER: Fifty percent of salaries.
OLIVER: But this list is just on on-air talent. That's not going to get you to fifty.
PETER: Every show has staff. Editors. Assistants. Producers.
OLIVER: Right. So, what about Andrew, we're not losing him, are we?
PETER: Andrew has been here forever.
OLIVER: Yeah, but didn't he hire you?
PETER: Is that what he's been telling you?
OLIVER: *Carter: Unfiltered* is a foundation for the evening schedule.
PETER: The ratings are abysmal.

He picks up Andrew's headshot.

OLIVER: We've got a terrible timeslot.
PETER: He doesn't podcast, he doesn't Substack. He's an ancient demographic.

He slaps the headshot on the whiteboard.

OLIVER: [*to audience*] Holy shit. If he cuts Andrew, I am dead.
PETER: I don't like him leaving the room.
Get him to sign an NDA, and gimme a cigarette.
OLIVER: Do you want an apple?
PETER: No, I need nicotine.
OLIVER: Is this a craving or a directive?
PETER: I need a Marlboro.
OLIVER: But you told me to keep them away from you.

PETER: I changed my mind.
OLIVER: You're giving up.
PETER: Don't be a smartarse!
OLIVER: Are you sure you want to do this?
PETER: I just fired a prick for posting cats! I need a cigarette, now.

OLIVER *offers a packet of Marlboros to* PETER.

PETER *takes the packet. It has one cigarette. He places it to his lips.*

Light.

OLIVER *takes a Zippo from his pocket.*

OLIVER: [*to audience*] To paraphrase Machiavelli, 'To defeat my enemy, I must become your enemy.' Or some shit like that.

OLIVER *holds the lighter close to the cigarette.*

PETER: You're shaking.
OLIVER: [*pretending to be emotional*] I'm sorry … This is very triggering for me.
PETER: Killers don't get emotional.
OLIVER: [*taking Andrew's headshot off the board*] You have got to save Andrew Carter.
PETER: Why do I have to do that?
OLIVER: [*flips the board*] Because Andrew Carter saved my life.

OLIVER *places Andrew's headshot on the blank whiteboard, alone.*

PETER: [*to audience*] And he tells me this origin story.

OLIVER *picks up the STORY mic. Music under the following.*

OLIVER: [*on mic*] My mother died of an overdose.

Found her on the kitchen floor. I was fourteen. I didn't know what to do.

Next day … I went to school, as if nothing had happened. I came home, I had nothing to eat. I started eating Friskies.

The cat food. For three weeks solid.

By the end of the month, the smell … The Friskies were all gone, and Mum was decomposing.

I ran away.
Stole some cars.
Got caught.
And then, I … I went to juvie.

OLIVER *is now close to Andrew's headshot.*

Six months later, this guy is doing a documentary on juvenile detention. He interviews a bunch of kids, and then he interviews me, all kinds of questions. The show goes to air.

I don't hear anything, so I write him a letter,

'Dear Mr Carter. I hope I'm not bothering you, but we don't have access to cable in detention. I'm just wondering, what did people think of me?'

And he writes back, and he says, 'I don't care what people think. In my world mate, everybody deserves another second chance.' When I got out, I came to see him.

PETER: … Did you tell him about the Friskies?

OLIVER: I didn't have to. He remembered me. He remembered me. Got me a cadetship. And here I am.

Andrew is more than a journo. He is a saint. And he deserves another, second chance.

OLIVER *lays down the STORY mic.* PETER *is silently gobsmacked.*

Peter? … Are you okay?

PETER *nods slowly.*

PETER: Good yarn.

OLIVER: [*to* PETER] Next?

PETER: [*meekly*] Wait …

PETER *moves to Andrew's headshot and puts a question mark.*

OLIVER: [*to audience*] My phone sounds an alert. [*To* PETER] It's time for your speech.

PETER: [*rattled*] … Already?

OLIVER: Yes. They are waiting for you.

PETER: I need a second.

OLIVER: Do you want me to tell them you're unwell—?

PETER: No. I just need to breathe.

ANDREW: [*off*] Blankey?

PETER *spins the whiteboard so* ANDREW *doesn't see his picture.*

[*Entering, re: blankets*] Got one for you … How did we finish up that discussion … ? You know, does Andrew Carter still have a job?

PETER: Now is not a great time.

ANDREW: Peter. Please.

PETER: Mate, good journos never beg.

OLIVER: [*to audience*] Peter disappears.

PETER *disappears.*

ANDREW: [*to audience*] And he sucks all of the oxygen out of the room.

THIRTEEN

OLIVER: 'Blankey'?! What are you doing? / What the fuck is wrong with you?

ANDREW: Okay, Oliver. Ollie! Listen to me, I just spoke to Frank Butcher.

OLIVER: You spoke to Frank?

ANDREW: Yes. He called me back from the Gold Coast.

And he sent pictures of the studio.

He shows OLIVER *pictures on his phone.*

And my god, it is horrific. This is our hell hole of destiny!

OLIVER: Wait a second, no! / … You are jumping to conclusions.

ANDREW: The pictures tell the story! Oliver! This is worse than 'Special Projects'!

This is the Abu Ghraib of newsrooms, and this is what loyalty gets you!

The only thing saving Frank is his contract, a golden bloody parachute—they couldn't afford to fire him!

OLIVER: You don't know all the details.

ANDREW *thrusts his phone to* OLIVER.

ANDREW: Read the bloody email!

OLIVER: [*reading the email*] 'Your golden parachute contract saved you from Centrelink.'

ANDREW: That's it. I am a dead man walking.

OLIVER: I need / you to calm down and listen to me.

ANDREW: I am dead! Dead, dead! I cannot listen; my brain is boiling! I am consumed by a terrible secret, and I simply must unburden myself.

OLIVER: Oh, god.

ANDREW: Look at me, look at *this face*! This used to be the serious face of serious journalism, in a flattering light.

Light softens on his face.

Thank you.

Back in the day, I was hot property with a positive trajectory.

One contract leads to the next, and the next and everything gets bigger and better and then, Cindy leaves me, I start 'channel-surfing', I lose my mojo, I got done for a DUI, and then my agent drops me.

OLIVER: Wo-ow!! No! I did not know that.

ANDREW: I know. I kept it quiet, and I refused to panic. I am a respected on-air talent, right? 'A journalist like me? I can take my pick of representation.'

I go out to market. There is some interest. I take some meetings.

But then, the phone stops ringing. It sits silent by my bed, like a pauper's grave at midnight. It's been twelve months, no new agent and now my contract has lapsed.

OLIVER: No agent and no contract?

ANDREW: That's right.

OLIVER: No golden parachute for us.

ANDREW: Not even close. Be hold …

Swings a blanket around his shoulders.

A new endangered species.

A walking corpse in a double Windsor knot.

A televisual vagrant! Oliver. We are a team. But right now, we are up shit creek in a Swiss cheese canoe. Little buddy. Please. I need some help.

OLIVER: Are you medically demented?

ANDREW: Sorry?

OLIVER: Is there something fucking mentally wrong with you? Are you drunk?

ANDREW: I'm not pissing in a cup, forget it!

OLIVER: Look at me! I am here. I am your producer!

ANDREW: I know who you are!

OLIVER: Have I been loyal to you?

ANDREW: What does that mean?

OLIVER: We are a team, and have I been loyal?

ANDREW: Not everything is all about you, Oliver—

OLIVER: I am very fucking loyal, Andrew, and I have been trying to help you all bloody night. You wanted to be the victim; I made you look like a victim! You needed a big story; I gave you a geomagnetic storm! A geomagnetic storm, Andrew! That's a potential extinction event but you don't want it, because 'no pictures'! I don't know what more I can do for you. Every second I am alive, every breath in my lungs, everything in me is dedicated to you! How can you not see this? I wrote a warning for you on the iPad—

ANDREW: I have no recollection of any warning.

OLIVER: Because you don't even know I'm alive!

OLIVER *shows* ANDREW *the iPad.*

In CAPS! Read this iPad back to me!

ANDREW: [*reading the iPad*] 'Suspicious activity, from a static IP, registered to California. They are dominating our hashtag! Peter is a nasty little fucker who cannot be trusted.' Oliver, you buried the lede, again. This is very disappointing. The story is: '*This nasty little fucker cannot be trusted.*' All this dribble about static IPs? Nobody understands that shit! Get the reader's attention, this is how a newsman writes a secret warning!

ANDREW *strides to the whiteboard and writes.*

'*Peter Francis* is a nasty little fucker who cannot be trusted.'
See?!

He emphasises on the board.

'Francis', '*nasty little fucker*' and 'trusted'.
This is the story. This is the … This is permanent marker.
'This nasty little fucker' is permanent marker. Oh fuck!

Chaos. ANDREW *runs to the door,* OLIVER *runs to whiteboard as—*

Get rid of it! Fucking hide it! Fucking! Flip it! Flip it!

OLIVER: Okay! Okay! Jesus! Andrew! Andrew, no! Flip it?!

ANDREW: Flip it!!

OLIVER: Flip it?

ANDREW: Fucking flip it!!

OLIVER *flips the whiteboard, to reveal Andrew's headshot alone.* ANDREW *is apoplectic.*

OLIVER: Do not freak out on me now!

ANDREW: Sweet mother of god!

OLIVER: Do not freak out! / Do not! Do not freak out on me now!

ANDREW: I cannot survive the Gold Coast! Kill me, just shoot me in the face!

OLIVER: You Boomers are so fucking fragile!

ANDREW: Okay, you crossed the line! I am not a Boomer. Gen X cusp. Fact.

OLIVER: Does the government send you a poo test?

ANDREW: That is personal, medical / information.

OLIVER: Have you got cash in your wallet?

ANDREW: Where else am I going to keep it?!

OLIVER: So you *do carry* a / wallet?

ANDREW: Oh ha, ha, very funny Mr Bit-con. /

OLIVER: Have you ever owned a typewriter? /

ANDREW: Everybody had a Golf Ball! /

OLIVER: Have you ever smoked on a plane?

ANDREW: Now, you listen to me, punk! When we started in this business, we could smoke anywhere we bloody wanted! In fact, we had to! It was mandatory, compulsory, it was part of the standard contract! We had to smoke at the desk, in the car, in the elevator, darkroom, lay out room, every interior you can possibly imagine! The world was a thin blue haze of filth and poison. Bars and pubs and trains and planes, it was insane, and it was beautiful! That was freedom of the press! When we were up against a deadline with nothing?! Or you're coming to the Slab and you're out of ideas?! Nicotine was there. The cigarette was the friend who steadied your hand. It was a horrific time, and—

ANDREW *places his headshot alongside the colleagues on the other side.*

We are in the trenches together!

OLIVER: None of this makes sense.

ANDREW: I am simply absorbing the horror of the reality of utter betrayal.

OLIVER: We have to talk about the elephant in this room. You and Peter are friends.

You shared lived experience.

You guys went through some shit. But there is a huge gap in this story.

I want to help you, I do, but I can't help you if you don't tell me everything.

The truth.

Beat.

You're not yourself.

You're a different man.

ANDREW: What I wouldn't give for an unfiltered Camel.

OLIVER: Andy. It's me. What happened to you?

Pause.

ANDREW: Pete was the best young reporter to ever walk in that door.

PETER *silently appears in the doorway and watches. He does not interrupt.*

Brian was on the lookout for young talent. On Wednesday afternoons, everybody with a shred of ambition, cadets, producers, journos would have a long lunch with the emperor. And Brian would shout the bar. Schooners of new and old war stories, cocaine, champagne and cigarettes, and if he liked you he would stand close. Perspiration. Alcohol. Pick your brain. Then we'd roll back here to the conference room to drink the wet cupboard dry, while we pitched him on the Slab. He would make you stand on the table and act out your idea. We were marionettes and if you were good, you got rewarded. If he didn't like you, it was brutal. The punishments. Humiliation.

Teach the boy a lesson.

Beat.

Cigarettes kill the taste.

Moment.

Welcome to the truth.

FOURTEEN

PETER: [*re: the insult on the whiteboard*] Who wrote that?

Long pause, then ...

[*Calmly*] Who wrote this shit about me?

ANDREW: [*to* OLIVER] Mate. Don't make it any worse for yourself.

PETER: Ando!

ANDREW: [*to* OLIVER] Looks pretty bad.

PETER: [*to* ANDREW] I recognise this handwriting! This / is you!

ANDREW: In fairness to me ... I have not had an original thought in a very long time. This is a transcription of existing IP.

PETER: We go back to the Ark, and this?

Beat.

I haven't seen your contract.

ANDREW: Paperwork, blah!

PETER: How many years left on your contract?

ANDREW: No, come / on mate. I'm sorry.

PETER: Oliver? ... Pull a copy of Ando's contract.

ANDREW *slaps the whiteboard.*

ANDREW: This is not *my opinion*; this is a transcript of what Oliver thinks.

OLIVER: / Whoa! That is crossing the line.

PETER: Who the hell are you?

ANDREW: You know who I am.

PETER: What kind of a man rescues a kid in juvie and tries to throw him under the bus?

ANDREW: What?

PETER: Oliver told me his origin story.

ANDREW: What origin are you talking about?

PETER: His mother. Died of an overdose.

OLIVER: Right, wait a second.

PETER: Decomposing on the kitchen floor.

ANDREW: Oliver, you told me you live with your mother. And she's a lovely, handsome woman—what the fuck is wrong with you?

PETER: He ate Friskies just to stay alive.

ANDREW: He fucking what?

PETER: Friskies.

ANDREW: He told you he ate Friskies?

PETER: The cat food.

ANDREW: I know what fucking Friskies are! / Oliver!

PETER: / Okay, calm down.

ANDREW: That is not your origin story to tell—

OLIVER: Yes and no—

ANDREW: No, no and no! The cat food is my story! You cannot just steal my Friskies, that is my life.

OLIVER: We work together, we are a team.

ANDREW: You are a filthy fucking Friskies liar!

OLIVER: I didn't lie, I just borrowed some fucking Friskies.

ANDREW: Young people cannot be trusted.

OLIVER: I was trying to build a narrative to save us, Andrew. You were young once!

ANDREW: But mate, I had integrity. We did. We still do.

OLIVER: Integrity? / Fuck me.

ANDREW: I live by a code of ethics!

OLIVER: You pricks crawled through garbage cans to put awards on the wall. You broke into people's houses. You tapped phones and downloaded voicemails, you fucked up people's lives, you murdered the truth, and you buried the facts in a shallow grave! How do you live with yourselves!

ANDREW: Hey! I am a human being; I have done bad; I have done good.

PETER: Oh, mate. You're being way too modest.

ANDREW: Thanks mate.

PETER: You've done a lot more bad than good.

ANDREW: You / fucking what? What are you saying?

PETER: You were a root-rat for an exclusive.

ANDREW: You wanna go? / You wanna have a go right now?

PETER: Shut up! Jesus, mate. You talk too much!

ANDREW: You are who you are because of me! I got you your first job.

PETER: Brian Mathews hired *me*, and you have never gotten over it.

ANDREW: I read the applications; I made the shortlist and sent my top five and what did he want to see? You best story, your CV? No. The headshots! The old fucker wanted the / faces.

PETER: He was looking for on-air talent.

ANDREW: And in all your time at RTN, when did you ever do a piece to camera?

PETER: I got my job on merit.

ANDREW: He wanted you on the Slab.

PETER: / You shut your mouth right now!

ANDREW: And you always worked as directed!

PETER *starts throwing the boxing gloves and pads at* ANDREW.

ANDREW *ducks and dives, tries to catch them, reaches for the 12.5kg dumbbell, tries to heave it at* PETER*! Almost dislocates his own shoulder!* OLIVER *announces!*

OLIVER: [*to all*] 'Brian Mathews' is trending!

PETER: Bloody fantastic! What's it look like?

OLIVER: It's a fucking car crash.

ANDREW *and* PETER *both retrieve their phones and check the socials.*

[*To audience*] The hashtag is doing its job and corralling accusations and allegations. Racist tendencies, extreme right-wing adoration, historic cocaine convictions and, there is so much traffic coming in from LA and okay, this is kicking off!

PETER: 'He did an epic amount of cocaine and behaved like Caligula.'

ANDREW: 'More blood in his nostrils than black caviar.'

OLIVER: 'A drunk, an addict, a predator. Hashtag Welcome to the Truth.'

ANDREW: Who posted that?

OLIVER: BoySixtyEight.

PETER: They want to be anonymous.

ANDREW: Can we follow and DM BoySixtyEight?

PETER: You want to fact-check a bot?

ANDREW: This could be a real person.

PETER: How many real people do you know with numbers in their name?

ANDREW: I am talking about the story, what is / their story?
OLIVER: [*to* ANDREW] We have to get this on air! Let's go!
ANDREW: No. What the hell is wrong with you?
OLIVER: No? … We're not going on air with this?
PETER: No.
OLIVER: [*to* PETER] You buried Colin for posting cats.
PETER: Cats are not going to sue us to death.
OLIVER: Peter, this is a massive story, and we are the epicentre. /
PETER: / Don't try to school me on the size of this thing?
ANDREW: No, this is not a story *yet*, it is a social media shitstorm.
PETER: Promoted by a horrific hashtag! /
OLIVER: 'Welcome to the Truth' is a bloody good hashtag, that's the truth.
ANDREW: 'Truth' is very subjective.
OLIVER: [*to* ANDREW] I want you in the studio now. Go get into make-up, let's go.
ANDREW: We don't have any pictures! / Television is a visual medium.
OLIVER: We have screenshots, and we have Brian Mathews in the flesh, out there!
PETER: Nobody is putting Brian on air.
OLIVER: Why not? / We've got the infrastructure to break this.
PETER: / What the fuck is wrong with you?
ANDREW: I am not going on air with rumour and gossip.
OLIVER: Right now, this is our exclusive. If we don't run it tonight, the competition will rip our guts out! This is our chance to get *Carter: Unfiltered* back on top.
ANDREW: Allegations do not win awards!
OLIVER: Yes, they fucking do!
PETER: They can—
OLIVER: They are our business model! Brian is out there right now, pissed as a frog in a pond. We can take him down tonight.
PETER: Predators belong in jail, but … /
OLIVER: You just put a 'but' in that sentence?
PETER: Predators belong in jail, but the defamation laws of this country protect them and defend them. Trust me, California Communications handles hundreds of clients just like Brian. Well-connected pedos with more money than god. If *you* go live with 'allegations', Brian

will lawyer up. He will engage a PR rehabilitation team and if he pays them enough money, I guarantee, by this time tomorrow, he will be the victim in this story.

ANDREW: He's right. It's true. You know how it works, Oliver.

Beat.

OLIVER: [*to* ANDREW] I thought you were tougher than this.

ANDREW: Hey. No. Fuck that. We do this old school, we dig in the weeds, we background, investigate, build a proper watertight story … And then when we know it's going to stick, we press 'Go' and we bury the prick.

OLIVER: No, we don't.

ANDREW: Mate! This is not some pissy podcast. / We have values, we have ethics!

OLIVER: Mate! I am your producer, and I need a serious journalist. Now!

PETER: Not going to happen.

OLIVER: I thought you were the hitman!

PETER: I don't have to answer to you!

OLIVER: Okay! Who is the 'boy', out there?

PETER: What are you talking about?

OLIVER: BoySixtyEight.

PETER: Why are you asking me?

OLIVER: He is the story. He knows the truth. Who is he, Peter? Who is BoySixtyEight?

PETER: That bot could be anybody.

OLIVER: You wanted all eyes on Brian.

PETER: Fifty years in media.

OLIVER: Does the boy live in California?

PETER: How the fuck should I know?

OLIVER: I think BoySixtyEight is you.

PETER: I am the consultant. I was hired to make the cuts / and this is what I am doing.

OLIVER: This is the story: the hitman came home to kill the / king!

PETER: Oliver! Email. Subject: Immediate Action Required! Brian. Effective immediately, your access to all company systems, premises, and resources is terminated. An internal investigation is active regarding multiple serious breaches of conduct, including criminal matters. The evidence is substantial. Understand: any attempt to contest this process will result in that evidence being made public. Vacate RTN property immediately. This directive is issued on the personal instruction of Christian Hardwick. Signed: Peter Francis. Director of News. Hardwick Holdings Pty Ltd. Send.

Beat.

Oliver, send.

OLIVER: How long have you been doing this?

PETER: Doing what?

OLIVER: Protecting Brian Mathews from potential prosecution?

PETER: Mate. This is not protection, this is the ultimate punishment.

OLIVER: Taking him off air is the ultimate punishment?

PETER: To kill a cunt like Mathews, you take away his microphone. Read that email back. He is going to disappear. He will! The emperor of outrage is a coward. Terrified of the truth. When he reads 'Peter Francis, Director of News' he's gonna have a fucking heart attack, he's going to announce he wants to 'spend more time with his family' and then he's going to die a lonely, quiet death. Irrelevant and forgotten.

OLIVER: And what about his victims?

ANDREW: Innocent people do not want to be dragged into the courts and thrust under the spotlight of cross examination—

PETER: And media speculation—

ANDREW: Just to prove what we know to be true.

OLIVER: What do you know to be true?

ANDREW: This is the business.

PETER: Send the email. Finish him.

OLIVER: You are protecting a predator.

ANDREW: / I have never protected a predator.

PETER: Nobody is protecting a predator.

OLIVER: So we do agree he is a 'predator'.

Beat.

PETER: Take that fucking hat off! Jesus! I told you!

OLIVER: This story is not going to die.

PETER: Are you serious? … / Are you really being serious, right now?

OLIVER: Yes, and when it breaks, when it breaks, the first question is going to be. 'How long have you known about the allegations of abuse?' /

PETER: Fuck off! /
OLIVER: That is the first question you're going to get.
ANDREW: From 'the media'?
OLIVER: The police.
PETER: We are not the criminals.
OLIVER: What did you do to stop him?
PETER: What did we / do?
ANDREW: We were kids.
OLIVER: I thought you were journalists.

OLIVER *picks up the recorder, like a hand grenade.*

PETER: Jesus Christ. / This is totally fucken crazy …
ANDREW: Okay, Ollie, mate! You win! You're right! We lead with the magnetic storm! Script it. Get it on the prompter! Let's go. The story is the 'end of the world'!

Beat.

Mate, you win. Come on. Please. I am directing you to do your job.
OLIVER: My job is to tell the story that some people want kept secret.
ANDREW: You walk out of here, you are not coming back.
OLIVER: And I can live with that. [*To audience*] And this is how it ends.

OLIVER *clicks the recorder off.*

He disappears.

PETER *and* ANDREW *wonder if* OLIVER *will return …*

Some kind of Shostakovich.

FIFTEEN

ANDREW: [*pulling his blanket closer*] What happened to loyalty?
PETER: Exactly …

PETER *wraps himself in a blanket.*

ANDREW: Did he record everything / that happened in here? …
PETER: Everything … Yes.
ANDREW: Fuck.
PETER: Yes … But did we, say anything …
ANDREW: Inappropriate?

PETER: Incriminating?
ANDREW: I don't think so.
PETER: He's not going to leak on us … Is he?
ANDREW: Are we still going woke, or … ?
PETER: You got any ciggies?
ANDREW: I could murder a Camel.

He gets whiskey for them both.

PETER: I'm out. I'm giving up.
ANDREW: How many times have you given up?
PETER: Lost count.
ANDREW: Worse than heroin.
PETER: Wish I never started.
ANDREW: Filthy habit.
PETER: Toxic. He even took my Luckies.
ANDREW: How'd he know about *them*?
PETER: Read my book.
ANDREW: So did I.

PETER *looks to* ANDREW.

Of course I did
PETER: What'd you think?
ANDREW: Good. But … I couldn't help noticing … I didn't rate a mention.
PETER: No.
ANDREW: And why is that?
PETER: Why do you think?

Beat.

ANDREW: If he goes to the cops or he uses that recording on his podcast …
PETER: Yep, yep. How do we play it?
ANDREW: Simple. We have to keep it simple.
PETER: Yes, but what do we do?
ANDREW: We do what we do best.
PETER: That's a fucken relief, I thought you were going say, 'come clean'.
ANDREW: Fuck, no. We create a story to sustain plausible deniability.

PETER: Great. So how do we start?

ANDREW: Well. Obviously, he quit in a rage. Or … maybe he get fired?

PETER: Yes! That's good. / Great.

ANDREW: Yes! He got fired for incompetence! The 'disgruntled former employee'.

PETER: Classic Gen Z archetype. Immature, with a bitter sense of entitlement.

ANDREW: Constantly pitching conspiracy theory stories, 'the sky is falling'.

PETER: He is a thief; he stole my cigarettes.

ANDREW: A thief and an alcoholic. He made us drink Doubles, all night.

PETER: And that was *after* the car crash. Don't forget the car crash.

ANDREW: I don't even have a licence. These are all facts.

PETER: *And* you were bleeding.

ANDREW: Yes. You tasted the blood …

PETER: PTSD and delayed concussion.

They smile. ANDREW *retrieves an emergency packet of Camels. They were taped under the plastic table this whole time.* PETER *is impressed. They both take a cigarette.*

ANDREW: We are the victims.

PETER: We kill it.

ANDREW: End of story.

PETER: Act of god.

They smile, then …

ANDREW: [*very quietly*] Welcome to the truth.

ANDREW *lights their cigarettes.*

Old-school West Coast sound, like Jackson Browne.

Snap to black.

THE END

#THIS IS NOT JOURNALISM

BY ROSS MUELLER

WRITTEN AND DIRECTED BY ROSS MUELLER
PRESENTED BY UPSTAGE AT THE PLAYHOUSE & AUSTRALIAN WRITERS THEATRE
CIVIC THEATRE PLAYHOUSE
26 SEPTEMBER — 4 OCTOBER 2025

Australian Writers Theatre proudly acknowledges the Awabakal and Worimi people as customary owners of the land on which we work and share our stories. We pay respects to elders past and present.

CAST IN ORDER OF APPEARANCE

JACK ANDREW OLIVER MADISON
MARK PEGLER ANDREW CARTER
PHILIP McGRATH PETER FRANCIS

CREATIVES

WRITER, DIRECTOR & SOUND DESIGN ROSS MUELLER
LIGHTING, PRODUCTION & STAGE DESIGN LYNDON BUCKLEY
DRAMATURG VANESSA BATES
ASSISTANT DIRECTOR & STAGE MANAGEMENT ANGELA ROBERTSON
COMMUNICATIONS & DIGITAL MARKETING ISABELLA MULLIGAN

RUNNING TIME 80-ish MINUTES NO INTERVAL
REC. AGES 16+ ADULT THEMES

This production was made possible by Upstage at the Playhouse, Civic Theatre, City of Newcastle, New Annual, and Creative Australia.

ABOUT AUSTRALIAN WRITERS THEATRE

AWT was founded by Ross Mueller in 2024. AWT is the first theatre brand to be solely dedicated to the Australian Writer/Director. The AWT mission is to promote, present and advocate for new writing, and new stories for the Australian stage. We are dedicated to the development of opportunities for Australian Writer/Directors.

ABOUT UPSTAGE AT THE PLAYHOUSE

Upstage at the Playhouse is an exciting initiative which has been developed by the Civic Theatre for City of Newcastle. The program aims to connect with the vibrancy and talent of our local theatre community by co-presenting and supporting works that showcase the ability and creativity of the Newcastle region.

WRITER/DIRECTOR NOTE

This is the first Australian Writers Theatre production.

#This Is Not Journalism was inspired by a conversation on a beach on New Years Day. It's hard to imagine a more Australian way to develop a concept for a new play, but of course, the journey from beach to presentation has been complex, challenging and enlightening.

#TINJ is essentially a real time play which uses comedy, tragedy, silence, amplification, funny noises and white board markers. It is all set in one night in the conference room of the fictitious Real Time News. It is not based on any one person living or dead and it is definitely not naturalism.

#TINJ has an ambition to dissect big themes in a small space, kind of like television. In the text and the rehearsal process we dug into masculinity, toxic behaviour, the legacy of legacy media and chaos of an unregulated, unedited new media landscape.

Fundamentally this play is about truth, story and facts. Those were the three words which guided the construction of the scenes. The characters know they can rewrite anything to accommodate their personal narrative. They can crisis manage their way out of the truth and assemble a narrative to promote their personal and political agendas.

In the first quarter of this century, we have entered a new looking glass of alternative facts. We have entered the final scene of legacy media, what happens next is a mystery, wrapped in a digital recorder, and delivered as podcast. This is how the news ends. Pretty funny stuff.

Many people have worked very hard to bring *#TINJ* to life, and I would like to thank each person who has provided support, insight, enthusiasm and encouragement. The Upstage program at Civic is an outstanding opportunity for the development of new works. Thank you to City of Newcastle, Leonie and Jordan, and Jo and the team in ticketing, marketing and tech support. Thank you also to Claire and Lucia at Currency Press, Catapult Dance for rehearsal support and Creative Australia.

It has been a pleasure and privilege to work with the cast and crew of creatives on this play. Special thanks to Mark, Phil, Jack, Vanessa, Angela, Isabella, Lyndon and Robert (the Captain Coach).

Hope you enjoy this story.

ROSS MUELLER

WRITER/DIRECTOR

ROSS MUELLER
WRITER/DIRECTOR/SOUND DESIGNER

Mueller is an Australian writer. His plays have been performed at Malthouse, MTC, STC, Griffin, La Mama, Red Stitch and ATYP. In 2024, The God Algorithm was shortlisted for best new play in the Australian Theatre Festival, New York City. In 2022, A SIMPLE ACT OF KINDNESS was nominated for most Outstanding New Writing in the Victorian Green Awards. In 2020, he was the winner of the Georgi Markov Award, BBC International Audio Drama Prize. He has had residences at New York New Dramatists in NYC and The Royal Court Theatre, London. He is founder and director of Australian Writers Theatre.

JACK ANDREW
OLIVER MADISON

Jack is a versatile performer with a wealth of experience. Professional credits include roles in AQUAMAN, PETER RABBIT 2, THE BIG DRY (Ensemble Theatre/ATYP), MASQUERADE (Griffin Theatre/Sydney Opera House), LA BOHEME (Opera Australia), THE UNLISTED (ABC ME/Netflix), PARSIFAL (Opera Australia). Newcastle credits include THE LARAMIE PROJECT (Lindsay St Players), CARMEN (Opera Hunter), DON'T MENTION CASABLANCA (Newcastle Theatre Company), 12 ANGRY MEN (Metropolitan Players), OLIVER (Newcastle Civic Theatre), NORMAL (Hunter Drama Actors Company), and THE ADDAMS FAMILY (The Very Popular Theatre Company).

MARK PEGLER
ANDREW CARTER

Civic Theatre Playhouse: THE MAGIC HOUR, CREATIVITY, AWAY, JOYRIDE. Atlantic Acting School: THE WOMEN (Off-Broadway). Sydney Festival: STICKY BRICKS. Commonwealth Games Cultural Festival: SWIMMING THE GLOBE. Sydney Fringe & New Annual: MAD BITCHES, THE LOU CHAPMAN SHOW. Cambodian Space Project: THE ROAD TO TIBOOBURRA. Zenith Theatre: Director CAT ON A HOT TIN ROOF, Assistant Director AFTER MAGRITTE AND THE REEL INSPECTOR HOUND. Perth Fringe & Darlinghurst Theatre: Director THE ANZAC LETTERS. Awards: World Monologue Games: Currently Ranked #1 in the world (Endurance) since 2022. Gold Medal Winner 2022 (A REAL THING), Bronze Medal Winner 2023 (RISE AND FALL OF THE FAIRY QUEEN). Newcastle Fringe: Best Newcastle Production 2023, Best Performance 2022 (THE LOU CHAPMAN SHOW). Training: Atlantic Acting School New York.

PHILLIP McGRATH
PETER FRANCIS

Philip started acting in the early 90's with the University of Newcastle. Since then, he has performed with many local theatre companies, among them Hunter Workers Theatre, All's One, Stray Dogs, Stooged, Upstage Theatre, Newcastle Theatre Company, Freewheels, Black Jack Theatre, The Very Popular Theatre Company, The Lowbrow Outfit, Metropolitan Players and Bearfoot Theatre. Phil has received 4 acting CONDAS for his work on local stages. He also has numerous appearances in low budget feature films, television dramas and national TVC's.

MARK PEGLER
ANDREW CARTER

Mark graduated from NIDA in 1984. Since then, Mark has appeared on stage for the State Theatre Company of South Australia, Sydney Theatre Company, Nimrod, Belvoir St, Melbourne Theatre Company, Playbox, Hothouse Theatre, Meryl Tankard's Australian Dance Theatre, numerous independent and commercial productions, as well as in film and television. Mark's recent work in Newcastle includes UNCLE VANYA for Her Productions and THE DARK ROOM for Stooged Theatre.

PHILLIP McGRATH
PETER FRANCIS

Philip started acting in the early 90's with the University of Newcastle. Since then, he has performed with many local theatre companies, among them Hunter Workers Theatre, All's One, Stray Dogs, Stooged, Upstage Theatre, Newcastle Theatre Company, Freewheels, Black Jack Theatre, The Very Popular Theatre Company, The Lowbrow Outfit, Metropolitan Players and Bearfoot Theatre. Phil has received 4 acting CONDAS for his work on local stages. He also has numerous appearances in low budget feature films, television dramas and national TVC's.

LYNDON BUCKLEY
LIGHTING & STAGE DESIGN

Lyndon is an Awabakal/Worimi (Newcastle) based Lighting Designer. He has won several City of Newcastle Drama Awards. Since leaving Hunter School of Performing Arts, he has worked on many productions across Australia including: Lighting Designer for The Very Popular Theatre Company: MARY POPPINS, JERSEY BOYS, PUFFS, CHESS. HER Productions: LOW LEVEL PANIC. Newcastle Theatre Company: THE EFFECT, A VIEW FROM A BRIDGE. Lulu Productions, THE MAGIC HOUR.

VANESSA BATES
DRAMATURG

Vanessa has dramaturged, script edited and taught playwrighting for several years. An award-winning playwright, Vanessa also writes for television and radio. Vanessa attained her Doctorate in Media Arts and Communication, examining mixed cultural identity and scriptwriting. Her plays include: THE MAGIC HOUR 2024, THE ONE, SMALL HARD TRUTHS, A GHOST IN MY SUITCASE, TRAILER, LIGHT BEGINS TO FADE, EVERY SECOND , THE MAGIC HOUR (2012), PORN.CAKE, CHECKLIST FOR AN ARMED ROBBER, and DARLING OSCAR. Vanessa won the Stoddart Playwriting Award, NSW Premier's Literary Award, AWGIE Awards, Inscription Chairman's Award, Inscription New Work Award, Paris Keesing residency and Varuna residency. She is a NIDA playwright studio graduate and a member of the playwrighting collective 7-ON which recently celebrated 20 years with the publication of 7-ON A COLLECTION. She is a founding Writer Director of Australian Writers Theatre.

ANGELA ROBERTSON

ASSISTANT DIRECTOR & STAGE MANAGEMENT

Angela Robertson (aka McKeown) is an award winning CONDA actress and director who has been working in the entertainment industry in both theatre and TV for over 25 yrs. Angela is a performance coach who has worked for CHAAYS talent agency, Hunter Drama and YPT with her own studio open locally for private lessons. Angela has enjoyed a wide variety of character roles, such as historical figure Gertrude Bell in AJAX IN IRAQ (Knock and Run). The traumatised wife, Stevie, in THE GOAT OR WHO IS SYLVIA (Chookas). Femme fatale Tanya in MAMMA MIA! (TVPTC 2019). She has also appeared in films by Rachel Ward and Jane Campion.

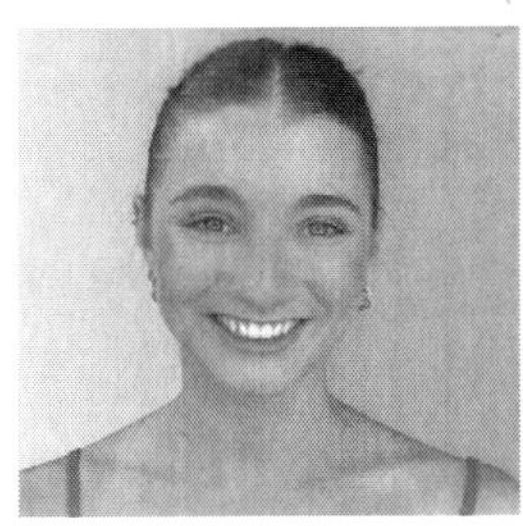

ISABELLA MULLIGAN

COMMUNICATION STRATEGIST & SOCIALS

Isabella Mulligan is the founder of By Bella Digital, a marketing agency helping small businesses build their brand story. She brings passion and strategy to every project, ensuring each brand connects authentically with its audience.